Spruce up your SPaG with CGP!

This fantastic CGP book is the best way to help pupils master Year 4 Spelling, Punctuation and Grammar.

It's packed with bite-sized bursts of practice at the perfect level for Year 4 pupils, and there's a fun puzzle at the end of each section.

We've included full answers to every question, and a handy progress chart to make marking a breeze!

What CGP is all about

Our sole aim here at CGP is to produce the highest quality books — carefully written, immaculately presented and dangerously close to being funny.

Then we work our socks off to get them out to you — at the cheapest possible prices.

Contents

Grammar

Grammar Test 1 2
Grammar Test 2 5
Grammar Test 3 8
Grammar Test 4 11
Grammar Puzzle 14

Punctuation

Punctuation Test 1 15
Punctuation Test 2 18
Punctuation Test 3 21
Punctuation Puzzle 24

Spelling

Spelling Test 1 25
Spelling Test 2 28
Spelling Test 3 31
Spelling Test 4 34
Spelling Test 5 37
Spelling Puzzle 40

Mixed Practice

Mixed Practice Test 1...41
Mixed Practice Test 2...44
Mixed Practice Test 3...47
Mixed Practice Test 4...50
Mixed Practice Puzzle 53

Answers..54
Progress Chart 62

Published by CGP

Editors: Keith Blackhall, Andy Cashmore, Emma Crighton, Catherine Heygate, Rebecca Russell, Adam Worster
With thanks to Michelle Rhodes and Holly Robinson for the proofreading.
With thanks to Jan Greenway for the copyright research.

ISBN: 978 1 78908 673 7
Clipart from Corel®
Printed by Elanders Ltd, Newcastle upon Tyne.
Based on the classic CGP style created by Richard Parsons.

Text, design, layout and original illustrations © Coordination Group Publications Ltd. (CGP) 2020
All rights reserved.

**Photocopying this book is not permitted, even if you have a CLA licence.
Extra copies are available from CGP with next day delivery • 0800 1712 712 • www.cgpbooks.co.uk**

Grammar Test 1

Warm up

1. Tick the box which points to the **verb** in the sentence below. Tick only **one** box.

   Linda feeds lettuce to her pet rabbit.
   ↑   ↑   ↑   ↑
   □   □   □   □

   _____
   1 mark

2. Underline the correct **determiner** to complete the sentence below.

   (That / An) shirt is far too big for you.

   _____
   1 mark

3. Tick the sentence below that is written in **Standard English**. Tick only **one** box.

   Do you know where we is? □

   They watches a film every weekend. □

   Fred was doing his maths homework. □

   _____
   1 mark

4. Underline the **adjective** in the sentence below.

   The youngest person here is Maria.

   _____
   1 mark

5. Complete each sentence below with the most suitable **preposition** from the box.

| until | under | with | on |

She slipped the message .... the door.

Aidan wanted to read the book .... me.

2 marks

6. Rewrite the sentences below so that they are in the **past progressive**. Only change **one** word in each sentence.

Hasan is making a cake.

....

They are looking at his shoes.

....

2 marks

7. Put a tick in each row to show whether the underlined clause is a **main clause** or a **subordinate clause**.

	Main Clause	Subordinate Clause
<u>Alison counted to ten</u> while everyone hid.		
<u>If we leave soon</u>, we'll get home before them.		

2 marks

8. Rewrite each sentence below, replacing the underlined words with a **pronoun**.

    I dropped the mug on the floor and <u>the mug</u> smashed.

    ....

    ....

    Lucy and Tom can't come because <u>Lucy and Tom</u> are ill.

    ....

    ....

    2 marks

9. Tick **two** sentences below which contain an **adverbial**.

He jumped higher than ever before.	☐
Ellie has a brand new skipping rope.	☐
Paul carried the plates very carefully.	☐
I wrote a long and interesting letter.	☐

    2 marks

END OF TEST

/ 14

Grammar Test 2

Warm up

1. Which word in the sentence below is a **proper noun**? Circle **one** box.

    The family went to France last year.

    | The | France | last |

    1 mark

2. Underline the correct option to complete the sentence in **Standard English**.

    Paula and (I / me) went to the zoo.

    1 mark

3. Fill in the gap in each sentence below with a suitable **possessive pronoun**.

    I own this house, so it is ....

    Julie gave him the marble — it was now ....

    2 marks

4. Underline the **noun phrase** in the sentence below.

    The narrow, windy road by the sea is lovely to drive on.

    1 mark

5. Tick **two** sentences below which are written in the **simple past** tense.

We have moved to another town. ☐

The fish had plenty to eat. ☐

Abdul was eating dinner. ☐

I drew a picture of a horse. ☐

2 marks

6. Join each pair of sentences using a suitable **conjunction**.

I like tennis. I like rugby.

....

....

We don't have cola. We'll have to drink lemonade.

....

....

2 marks

7. Complete the sentence below by adding an **adverbial**.

.... , I walked home.

1 mark

8. Put a tick in each row to show whether the word in **bold** is being used as a **subordinating conjunction** or a **preposition**.

	Subordinating Conjunction	Preposition
I'll see Christa **after** I finish my homework.		
We don't eat pudding **before** dinner.		

2 marks

9. Write down what the **pronouns** in **bold** below refer back to.

The twins watch a film. **They** think **it** is exciting.

They refers back to ....

It refers back to ....

2 marks

END OF TEST

/ 14

Grammar Test 3

> **Warm up**
>
> 1. Rewrite the **verb** in **bold** so that it is in the correct **tense**.
>
>   Nick went to his bedroom and **tidies** away his toys.
>
>   ....
>
>   1 mark
>
> 2. Circle the missing **determiner** from the sentence below.
>
>   .... weather was awful yesterday.
>
> | A | | An | | The |
>
>   1 mark

3. Underline the correct option to complete each sentence in **Standard English**.

   Nadia gave (them / these) some presents.

   Harry really likes (them / these) teacups.

   2 marks

4. Complete the sentence below with a suitable **adverb**.

   The woman was singing .... loudly.

   1 mark

5. Tick the sentence below that is in the **present progressive**. Tick only **one** box.

Sharks live in the ocean. ☐

They are working hard. ☐

Layla was visiting Jeff. ☐

1 mark

6. Underline the **preposition phrase** in each sentence below.

The river flowed under the bridge.

After lunch, they had a long nap.

2 marks

7. In the sentence below, what **word class** does the underlined word belong to? Circle **one** box.

This is the field where Joel plays football.

| pronoun | determiner | adjective | noun |

1 mark

8. Underline the **noun phrase** in the sentence below.
   Then write the **noun** on the line.

   Our very cute puppy barked cheerfully.

   Noun: ....

   2 marks

9. Rewrite the sentence below in **Standard English**.

   They goes outside but Oliver stays indoors.

   ....

   ....

   1 mark

10. Tick **two** sentences where the underlined
    words are a **subordinate clause**.

    <u>Mya will bake a cake</u> for my birthday.   ☐

    Callum wrote poems <u>when he was younger</u>.   ☐

    <u>Before I go home</u>, I need to go to the shop.   ☐

    It's going to be <u>a sunny day tomorrow</u>.   ☐

    2 marks

    END OF TEST

    / 14

Grammar Test 4

Warm up

1. In the sentence below, what **word class** does the underlined word belong to? Circle **one** box.

   Laura's parrot is incredibly <u>funny</u> when it talks.

   | verb | adverb | adjective | preposition |

   1 mark

2. Underline the **determiner** in the sentence below.

   I have sent many postcards today.

   1 mark

3. Tick the sentence below that is written in the **simple present** tense. Tick only **one** box.

   Todd is going to the dentist. ☐

   Rina likes playing the drums. ☐

   We believed the ghost story. ☐

   1 mark

4. Circle the **possessive pronoun** below.

   them   theirs   her   Hugh's

   1 mark

5. Underline the correct option to complete the sentence in **Standard English**.

We could (have / of) gone to the seaside instead.

1 mark

6. Complete each sentence below with the most suitable **conjunction** from the box.

| unless   because   although |

We were late .... we overslept.

.... she was full, Jill still made a pizza.

2 marks

7. Put a tick in each row to show whether the words are a **noun phrase** or a **preposition phrase**.

	Noun Phrase	Preposition Phrase
an enormous hippo		
over the fence		
before sunset		

3 marks

8. Rewrite the following so that they are in the **present perfect**.

   Kabir cleans ....

   We dance ....

   2 marks

9. Rewrite each sentence below using **Standard English**.

   I ain't got any more peaches.

   ....

   ....

   Kim doesn't know nothing about monkeys.

   ....

   ....

   2 marks

END OF TEST

/ 14

Grammar Puzzle

This puzzle is a brilliant way to practise your grammar skills.

Pyramid Puzzler

Circle the letter next to the correct answer to each question. Write the letters you've circled in the boxes to spell out the code word that opens the pyramid.

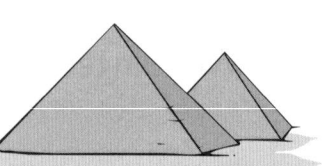

1 Which phrase below is an **adverbial**?

the small yellow boat — **R**
first thing in the morning — **S**
a fun-filled weekend — **B**

2 Which of these sentences uses **Standard English**?

You should of seen it. — **E**
You should have seen it. — **U**

3 Which word in this sentence is a **possessive pronoun**?
The hat he wore was mine.

The — **C**
he — **R**
mine — **N**

4 What is the word '**during**' an example of?

adjective — **G**
preposition — **S**
adverb — **A**

5 Which of these examples is a **subordinate clause**?

until it got dark — **E**
they played outside — **A**

6 Which two **pronouns** could replace the nouns in this sentence?
Grace thinks camels are cute.

She, they — **T**
She, it — **S**
Her, they — **R**

The code word is: | 1 | 2 | 3 | 4 | 5 | 6 |

Grammar Puzzle   14   © CGP — not to be photocopied

Punctuation Test 1

Warm up

1. Underline the word that should have an **apostrophe**.

   I still havent managed to find the toys I lost earlier.

   1 mark

2. Tick the sentence that is punctuated **incorrectly**. Tick only **one** box.

   Have you seen that new action film? ☐

   That unicyclist was absolutely incredible? ☐

   Katlego and Jim have been at the park all day. ☐

   1 mark

3. Tick **two** boxes to show where the **inverted commas** should go.

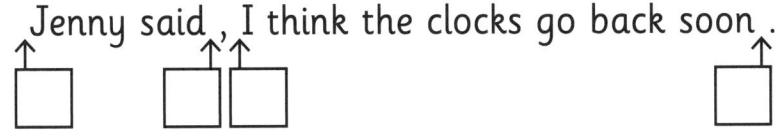

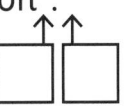

   Jenny said , I think the clocks go back soon .

   1 mark

4. Underline **two** words that should start with a **capital letter**.

   Keshav recently visited Marco in rome. They hadn't met up since Marco left england seven years ago.

   2 marks

5. Rewrite the sentence below, adding a **comma** in the correct place.

   Yesterday evening I went to the theatre.

   ....

   ....

   1 mark

6. Tick the sentence that uses an **apostrophe** correctly.
   Tick only **one** box.

   My mountain bike is on it's last legs. ☐

   It's finally going to snow tonight. ☐

   The spider thought it's web was lovely. ☐

   1 mark

7. Rewrite the sentence below, adding **commas** in the correct places.

   Maya spent the day swimming in streams walking through woods sketching birds and listening to music.

   ....

   ....

   ....

   2 marks

Punctuation Test 1

8. Rewrite the sentence below, correcting **two** punctuation errors.

we are going to Tracys birthday party this weekend.

....

....

2 marks

9. Put **two paragraph markers** (//) in the passage below to show where new paragraphs should start.

> Bears are impressive creatures, and many people find them fascinating. As a result, they often appear in myths and stories. Polar bears are among the largest bears. They live in the Arctic Circle where they hunt both on land and in the sea. Kodiak bears are also large and can weigh more than 650 kg. They live on a group of islands near Alaska. Unlike polar bears, they eat plants as part of their diet.

2 marks

10. Circle the most appropriate **heading** for the passage in question 9.

| What Bears Eat | Dangerous Bears | All About Bears |

1 mark

END OF TEST

/ 14

Punctuation Test 2

Warm up

1. Circle **one** word that should start with a **capital letter**.

   they think I won't be able to make this jump.

   1 mark

2. Tick the sentence that is likely to end with an **exclamation mark**. Tick only **one** box.

   Don't you want to swim ☐

   This is utterly delicious ☐

   I don't think I'll go running ☐

   1 mark

3. Write the items in the boxes into a **sentence**, using **commas** in the correct places.

   | a bag of radishes | two floppy hats | nine bottles of ketchup | and some pink pens |

   I need to buy ....

   ....

   ....

   2 marks

4. Write the correct punctuation mark in each box below.

   Did Liam win his chess match earlier ☐

   Stacey wants to go shopping this week ☐

   How can we try to solve this problem ☐

   3 marks

5. Underline **one** word that should have an **apostrophe**.
   Write out the word on the line below **with** an apostrophe.

   The three cats water bowls always seem to be empty.

   ....

   2 marks

6. Put **inverted commas** in the correct places in the sentence below.

   I'm going to watch the stars , said Zinhle .

   Why have **inverted commas** been used in this sentence?

   ....

   ....

   2 marks

7. Add **one comma** to each sentence below.

   Because of the old milk it smells bad in here.

   If the rain stops the cricket might start again.

   2 marks

8. Read the passage below.

   > Percy the Pirate of Peterborough was nearing the end of his epic treasure hunt. He'd spent years studying maps, visiting deserted islands and solving puzzles, and now his moment was here. All he had to do was solve the devilishly difficult final puzzle.
   >
   > Sweat dripped down his face as he looked at the final piece. Was he right? Suddenly, he wasn't sure.

   Write a suitable **heading** for this text.

   ....

   1 mark

END OF TEST

/ 14

Punctuation Test 3

Warm up

1. This sentence is missing one **comma**.
   Put it in the correct box.

   Beth bought ☐ a frisbee ☐ shoes and a ☐ hat.

   1 mark

2. Tick the sentence that uses **capital letters** correctly. Tick only **one** box.

   In June, I will go to india with my parents. ☐

   We like to play Football with Emily. ☐

   It is Tilly's birthday party next Wednesday. ☐

   1 mark

3. Shorten these words using an **apostrophe**.

   would not .... we will ....

   2 marks

4. Tick the sentence that uses **apostrophes incorrectly**. Tick only **one** box.

   Aneesa's history project was amazing. ☐

   The dog's tail wagged all day. ☐

   Nigels' eyes were wide with shock. ☐

   1 mark

5. Draw lines to match each sentence to the missing punctuation mark.

She likes to travel

Do you think Kate is funny

What a brilliant show that was

.

!

?

2 marks

6. Circle the correct options to complete the sentences below.

The panda always eats all of (it's / its) bamboo.

Mary thinks (it's / its) going to rain today.

2 marks

7. Rewrite the sentence below, correcting **three** punctuation errors.

before the sun came up Azgar went for a run

....

....

3 marks

8. Read the passage below.

> Despite its incredible height, people have been trying to climb Mount Everest since 1922. The first successful climb was in 1953, when Edmund Hillary and Tenzing Norgay became the first people to stand on top of the world.

Write a suitable **heading** for this text.

....

1 mark

9. Rewrite the sentence below, adding **inverted commas** in the correct places.

We've been walking for absolutely ages, moaned Mark.

....

....

1 mark

END OF TEST

/ 14

Punctuation Puzzle

This puzzle is a brilliant way to practise your punctuation skills.

Baffling Bags

Five spies have lost their bags. Can you work out who each bag belongs to? Count the number of punctuation mistakes in each spy's message. The number of mistakes matches the number on their bag.

Lara
My bag doesnt contain any secret plan's, special gadgets or, jam jars.

Luke
what is my bag like. Its got a hidden pocket, at the bottom that is full of grapes".

Satoshi
After sunset my bag becomes invisible. This means it won't be stolen while I am asleep.

Maeve
What a great bag I have? Itll play music to me if I say the secret word.

Petra
My bag has a parachute This is great, when Im' on an Aeroplane.

Can you write down who each bag belongs to?

Spelling Test 1

Warm up

1. Circle **one** word below that is spelt correctly.

   | notise | city | fansy | silense |

   1 mark

2. Underline **one** spelling mistake in the sentence below.

   Sunita had troubel deciding which socks to wear.

   1 mark

3. Add a **prefix** to the word in **bold** so that the sentence means the **opposite**.

   The puppy ....**behaved** all day.

   1 mark

4. Underline the correct option to complete the sentence below.

   I would've (prefered / preferred) to go to the beach.

   1 mark

5. Draw lines to match each word beginning to the correct ending.

plea..........

na...........

enclo........

sure

ture

3 marks

6. Tick the sentence below which contains a spelling mistake. Tick only **one** box.

Mike's cunning scheme worked. ☐

My mum is the best baker in town. ☐

I love hearing my voice eko. ☐

1 mark

7. Rewrite the sentence below, correcting the spelling of the word in **bold**.

Millie won first prize in the school **sience** contest.

....

....

1 mark

Spelling Test 1   26   © CGP — not to be photocopied

8. Write the correct spelling of the words in **bold** below.

Let's have a **discushion**. ....

The **politisian** smiled. ....

Her **expresion** changed. ....

3 marks

9. Underline **two** spelling mistakes in the passage below.

> Danny's sister, Julia, had always urged him to stay out of the attic. She claimed that there was a dangereous ghost lurking up there.
>
> One day, Danny decided to creep up to the attic to investigate. Although he felt nervous, he was also cureous to see what the ghost looked like.

2 marks

END OF TEST

/ 14

Spelling Test 2

Warm up

1. Tick the word below which is spelt **incorrectly**.
   Tick only **one** box.

   clapping ☐   replying ☐   closeing ☐

   1 mark

2. Underline **one** spelling mistake in the sentence below.

   Zuko was allways the tallest student at school.

   1 mark

3. Draw lines to match each word to the correct **silent letter**.

   ………nuckle   g

   ………nat   k

   1 mark

4. Rewrite each word below, adding the prefix 'im' or 'in'.

   possible   ……………………………

   active   ……………………………

   2 marks

5. Rewrite the sentence below, correcting the spelling of the word in **bold**.

The thief managed to steal the expensive **anteek** clock.

....

....

1 mark

6. Tick **two** sentences below which contain a spelling mistake.

The farmer weighed her pumpkins. ☐

The veyns in my arm are blue. ☐

Thay finished the quiz very quickly. ☐

The freight train arrived at the station. ☐

2 marks

7. Rewrite the words below as adverbs using the suffix '**ly**'. You may need to change the spelling of the root word.

| final | .... |

| dramatic | .... |

2 marks

8. Underline the correct option to complete each sentence below.

The (piramids / pyramids) in Egypt are ancient.

Steve knows so much about Greek (myths / miths).

2 marks

9. Rewrite the passage below, correcting the **two** spelling mistakes.

Freddie was full of admirashion for his amazing friends. They had helped him with the preparasions for his wonderful party.

....

....

....

....

....

2 marks

END OF TEST

/ 14

Spelling Test 3

Warm up

1. Underline the correct word to complete the sentence below.

    I'm going to (where / wear) my favourite coat tonight.

    1 mark

2. Tick the sentence which contains a spelling mistake. Tick only **one** box.

    Sophie is an excellent squash player. ☐

    I knew I'd bought the wrong quontity. ☐

    Miles ran away from the angry swan. ☐

    1 mark

3. Circle the letter or group of letters that is missing from **all** the words below.

    t......ch   c......sin   c......ntry

    | ouh | u | ou |

    1 mark

4. Underline **one** word that is spelt **incorrectly**.

    limitting   regretting   directing

    1 mark

5. Circle **two** words where '**ch**' makes the hard '**c**' sound.

scholar   chalet

brochure   machine

chute   chorus

2 marks

6. Draw lines to match each word beginning to the correct ending.

confu..........   **tion**

posse............   **sion**

opera........   **ssion**

2 marks

7. Rewrite the sentence below, correcting the spelling of the word in **bold**.

There will be a **cresent** moon tonight.

....

....

1 mark

8. Underline the correct option to complete each sentence below.

I carefully wrote the (adress / **address**) on the envelope.

We'll (probly / **probably**) go for a swim later.

It's hard to (**describe** / discribe) how delicious it was.

3 marks

9. Rewrite the sentences below, correcting **two** spelling mistakes.

As soon as school was over, Amina and her friends raced to the leiture centre. They couldn't wait to try out the new advensure playground.

....

....

....

....

2 marks

END OF TEST

/ 14

Spelling Test 4

Warm up

1. Tick the word that is spelt **incorrectly**.

   The animals cheer up the patients in the hospitel.
   ↑   ↑   ↑   ↑
   □   □   □   □

   1 mark

2. Underline **one** spelling mistake in the sentence below.

   Deb broke her rist when she fell out of the tree.

   1 mark

3. Write the correct spelling of the word in **bold** on the line below.

   Zoe's football team is at the top of the **leage**.

   ....

   1 mark

4. Circle the group of letters that is missing from the word in **bold**.

   The **electri**......... had found the problem.

   | sian | | cian | | tion |

   1 mark

Spelling Test 4 — 34 — © CGP — not to be photocopied

5. Rewrite the words below, adding the suffix '**ous**'.
   You may need to change the spelling of the root words.

   | glamour | .... |

   | envy | .... |

   2 marks

6. Underline **one** spelling mistake in the sentence below.
   Then rewrite the sentence, correcting the mistake.

   He believes there will be an alien invassion tomorrow.

   ....

   ....

   1 mark

7. Use the **prefixes** in the box to complete the sentences below. You should only use each prefix once.

   | re   auto   anti |

   The vet gave my rabbit some ....biotics.

   Eve decided to ....decorate the kitchen.

   I want to read the actor's ....biography.

   2 marks

8. Underline the words below that are spelt **incorrectly**.
Then write the correct spellings on the dotted lines.

forgotten   canceling   permitted   remaining

fastening   deposited   marketing   profitted

....

....

2 marks

9. Underline **three** spelling mistakes in the passage below.

"It's not fare," Lena muttered with a groan. "It's pouring with rain and I can hardly see a thing through the missed. Why is the whether always terrible when we're on holiday?"

3 marks

END OF TEST

/ 14

Spelling Test 5

Warm up

1. Underline the correct option to complete the sentence below.

    There is (nothing / nuthing) but jam in the cupboards.

    1 mark

2. Tick the sentence below which contains a spelling mistake. Tick only **one** box.

    Indira likes to wear lots of sparkly jewellery. ☐

    Mick bought me some fudge for my birthday. ☐

    My uncle lives in a small villadge in Scotland. ☐

    1 mark

3. Draw lines to match each **prefix** to the correct word.

    | il | relevant |
    | im | legal |
    | ir | perfect |

    2 marks

4. Add '**g**' or '**gue**' to the sentences below so that they are spelt correctly.

   The giraffe had a surprisingly long ton............... .

   Matt put whipped cream onto the merin............... .

   The alarm went off and I spran............... out of bed.

   3 marks

5. Underline **one** spelling mistake in the sentence below. Then rewrite the sentence, correcting the mistake.

   I have trouble sitting still — I'm always fidgetting.

   ....

   ....

   1 mark

6. Underline **two** spelling mistakes in the passage below.

   My friend Barry has an amazing imagineation. He's always writing extraordinaryly exciting stories. I think he will be a famous author one day.

   2 marks

7. Circle the word where '**ch**' is pronounced '**sh**'.

    | character | moustache | mechanic |

    1 mark

8. Write down **one** other word where '**ch**' is pronounced '**sh**'.

    ....

    1 mark

9. Rewrite the sentences below, correcting the spelling of the words in **bold**.

    Christine **desided** to sleep in her tent.

    ....

    ....

    The robin is a **reguler** visitor to Nick's garden.

    ....

    ....

    2 marks

END OF TEST

/ 14

Spelling Puzzle

This puzzle is a brilliant way to practise your spelling skills.

Word Bank Robbery

Neil has stolen some words and replaced them with incorrectly spelt words. Circle ten words below that are spelt incorrectly, then find the correct spellings of these words hidden in the word search.

Watch out — there are some incorrectly spelt words hidden in the word search too!

The words in the word search may be written across, down, backwards or diagonally.

sckeme

dubble

invasion

Febuary

happily

gentley

century

promiss

couragous

mashine

speshial

guard

ordinery

preparacion

immature

```
F E B U A R Y I O Z D S
E C M A C H I N E K O C
B H O I M A T U R E U H
R A P U O C K L A N B E
U P A P R O M I S E L M
A P R T E A M D H I E E
R Y G B A L G E N T L Y
Y L Q F X D K E J B A G
C Y R A N I D R O F N N
S P E C I A L O E U V W
I L R A Y R U T N E S I
D P R E P A R A T I O N
```

Spelling Puzzle   © CGP — not to be photocopied

Mixed Practice Test 1

Warm up

1. Circle **one** word below that is spelt **incorrectly**.

   | flung | | yung | | couple |

   1 mark

2. Tick the sentence below that uses **commas** correctly. Tick only **one** box.

   If we score again, we will win the match. ☐

   Eliza is baking a pie, for her friend. ☐

   I have to go home, when it gets dark. ☐

   1 mark

3. Tick to show which **possessive pronouns** are missing from the sentences below. Tick only **one** box.

   Vicky's painting is a lot neater than ....

   .... is more colourful as well.

   yours and **Hers** ☐

   she and **Yours** ☐

   you and **Hers** ☐

   1 mark

4. Rewrite the sentences below so that they are in the **present progressive**.

Zack builds a boat.

....

They wash the car.

....

2 marks

5. Rewrite the words below as nouns using the suffix '**ation**'. You may need to change the spelling of the root word.

| inform | .... |

| adore | .... |

2 marks

6. Underline **one** word that should have an **apostrophe**. Write out the word on the line below **with** an apostrophe.

Itll be amazing to see the turtles!

....

2 marks

7. Put a tick in each row to show whether the sentence contains a **subordinating conjunction** or a **co-ordinating conjunction**.

	Subordinating Conjunction	Co-ordinating Conjunction
I am tired but I need to stay awake.		
John will stay here until I pick him up.		

2 marks

8. Underline the words below that are spelt **incorrectly**. Then write the correct spellings on the dotted lines.

invention   tenssion   confession

musician   action   injectsion

magisian   permission   completion

....

....

....

3 marks

END OF TEST

/ 14

Mixed Practice Test 2

Warm up

1. Underline **one** spelling mistake in the sentence below.

   This car is one of a kind — it's completely uniqe.

   1 mark

2. Tick the sentence that uses **capital letters** correctly. Tick only **one** box.

   I can't believe it is snowing in march! ☐

   On Tuesday, we are visiting a farm. ☐

   France is a Country and Paris is a City. ☐

   1 mark

3. In the sentence below, what **word class** does the underlined word belong to? Circle **one** box.

   Manny's father rides around on a <u>green</u> scooter.

   | adverb | preposition | adjective | verb |

   1 mark

4. Underline the **pronoun** in the sentence below.

   Yui told him to come home right away.

   1 mark

5. Add **commas** to the list below.

   Nimit wants to hike up a mountain go to a llama farm play crazy golf and eat some crisps.

   2 marks

6. Tick **two** noun phrases below which contain **preposition phrases**.

   Amanda's fossil on the shelf ☐

   the extremely tall oak tree ☐

   my brother's tiny, bouncing rabbit ☐

   our secret entrance behind the wall ☐

   2 marks

7. Draw lines to match each sentence to the missing letters.

The lioness hunted her pr............ .	eigh
An octopus has ....t legs.	ei
The king r............gned for a long time.	ey

   2 marks

8. Circle the word that needs an **apostrophe** in the sentence below.

The bears are eating the campers food.

1 mark

9. Rewrite the sentence below so that it starts with the **adverbial**. Remember to use the correct punctuation.

Nina rides her motorbike every evening.

....

....

1 mark

10. Rewrite the sentences below, correcting **two** spelling mistakes.

Shane loves to exersise. He regularly runs through the centre of town to the libery and back again.

....

....

....

2 marks

END OF TEST

/ 14

Mixed Practice Test 2

Mixed Practice Test 3

Warm up

1. Circle the group of letters that is missing from **all** the words below.

   e............   do............   fri............

   | ge | | je | | dge |

   1 mark

2. Put the correct punctuation mark in the box below.

   How much longer do we have to wait ☐

   1 mark

3. Rewrite the words below, adding the suffix '**er**'.
   You may need to change the spelling of the root word.

   | control | ....

   | command | ....

   2 marks

4. Underline the **determiner** in the sentences below.

   Have you seen my book anywhere?

   There are some letters here for Eva.

   2 marks

5. Underline the **subordinate clause** in the sentence below.

Tony plays the piano when he stays with his uncle.

1 mark

6. Add **inverted commas** to the sentence below.

Kieran said , I'm going to plant a tree .

1 mark

7. Put **two** paragraph markers (//) in the passage below to show where new paragraphs should start.

> The ice cream parlour serves lots of flavours. You can get blackcurrant, bubblegum and even cabbage! They're all very tasty. Last week, I went to the parlour, but it was closed. I had forgotten that they're shut during the winter. When I am older, I will have my own ice cream parlour. It'll be open all year and will serve hot chocolate during the winter.

2 marks

8. Add an **adjective** and a **preposition phrase** to the word below to make a **noun phrase**.

the .... elephant ....

....

2 marks

9. Rewrite the sentence below, correcting **two** spelling mistakes.

Jason asked Nat to help him meature his furniture, a treasure chest and a brown picsure frame.

....

....

....

2 marks

END OF TEST

/ 14

Mixed Practice Test 4

Warm up

1. Tick the sentence below that uses **determiners** correctly. Tick only **one** box.

   This cars are all very expensive. ☐

   We can hear every strange noises. ☐

   I still have many letters to hand out. ☐

   1 mark

2. Tick the word which is spelt **incorrectly**. Tick only **one** box.

   history ☐   misery ☐   mistery ☐

   1 mark

3. Complete the sentence below with a suitable **prefix**.

   Sally and Bilal often argue and ....agree.

   1 mark

4. Circle the correct option to complete each sentence in the **present perfect**.

   Barney (have / has) talked to his children.

   We (had / have) eaten all of the broccoli.

   2 marks

5. Underline the correct option to complete the sentence below.

   The bird is looking at (its / it's) chicks.

   1 mark

6. Rewrite the words below as adverbs using the suffix '**ly**'. You may need to change the spelling of the root word.

   horrible + ly → ....

   usual + ly → ....

   2 marks

7. Draw lines to match each **paragraph** to the most suitable **subheading**.

   | During the trip, you'll have the chance to try archery, kayaking and a zip wire. |

   | Superb Campsite |

   | Our site has everything. We provide cosy tents and there are clean bathrooms nearby. |

   | Fun Activities |

   | The trip is now just half price. That includes your food and equipment. |

   | Affordable Deals |

   2 marks

8. Rewrite the sentences below in **Standard English**.

Harriet should of passed the ball to me.

....

....

I've got to put all them books away.

....

....

2 marks

9. Underline **two** spelling mistakes in the passage below.

I had to go to the kemist after eating lunch at Gemma's house because her food made me ill. I was surprised because Gemma's a famous shef. She was very sorry.

2 marks

END OF TEST

/ 14

Mixed Practice Puzzle

This puzzle is a brilliant way to practise your spelling, punctuation and grammar skills.

Dani's Dilemma

In the ruins of an ancient city, Dani the Diver has found a mysterious locked door, but she needs a code to open it. Help Dani find the code by answering the questions below. Then, write your answers in the boxes at the bottom of the page to open the door.

How many conjunctions are there in this box?

You have found the mermaids' door, but can you open it? Many have tried to solve the puzzle and failed. If you wish to succeed, read our story.

How many of the words in this box are spelt incorrectly?

Behind this door is an inmortality potion. We maid it for an impatient dragon who promised us tremendus powers. When she grew tired of waiting, she angryly blew our city to pieces with one mighty breathe.

How many words in this box need apostrophes?

The dragons powerful, but she isnt smart enough to unlock the door. Its time to see if you have managed to uncover the mermaids secret.

The code to unlock the door is: ☐ ☐ ☐

Answers

Grammar Test 1 – pages 2-4

1. Linda feeds lettuce to her pet rabbit.
   ↑
   ✓
   (**1 mark**)

2. <u>That</u> shirt is far too big for you.
   (**1 mark**)

3. Fred was doing his maths homework.
   (**1 mark**)

4. The <u>youngest</u> person here is Maria.
   (**1 mark**)

5. She slipped the message **under** the door.
   Aidan wanted to read the book **with** me.
   (**1 mark for 1 correct,
   2 marks for both correct**)

6. Hasan was making a cake.
   They were looking at his shoes.
   (**1 mark for 1 correct,
   2 marks for both correct**)

7.
	Main Clause	Subordinate Clause
<u>Alison counted to ten</u> while everyone hid.	✓	
<u>If we leave soon</u>, we'll get home before them.		✓

   (**1 mark for 1 correct,
   2 marks for both correct**)

8. I dropped the mug on the floor and **it** smashed.
   Lucy and Tom can't come because **they** are ill.
   (**1 mark for 1 correct,
   2 marks for both correct**)

9. He jumped higher than ever before.
   Paul carried the plates very carefully.
   (**1 mark for 1 correct,
   2 marks for both correct**)

Grammar Test 2 – pages 5-7

1. France
   (**1 mark**)

2. Paula and <u>I</u> went to the zoo.
   (**1 mark**)

3. I own this house, so it is **mine**.
   Julie gave him the marble — it was now **his**.
   (**1 mark for 1 correct,
   2 marks for both correct**)

4. <u>The narrow, windy road by the sea</u> is lovely to drive on.
   (**1 mark**)

5. The fish had plenty to eat.
   I drew a picture of a horse.
   (**1 mark for 1 correct,
   2 marks for both correct**)

6. E.g. I like tennis **and** I like rugby.
   E.g. We don't have cola **so** we'll have to drink lemonade.
   (**1 mark for each sentence that uses a sensible conjunction, up to 2 marks in total**)

7. E.g. **After the film**, I walked home.
   (**1 mark for any sensible adverbial**)

8.
	Subordinating Conjunction	Preposition
I'll see Christa **after** I finish my homework.	✓	
We don't eat pudding **before** dinner.		✓

   (**1 mark for 1 correct,
   2 marks for both correct**)

9. **They** refers back to **the twins**.
   It refers back to **the film**.
   (**1 mark for 1 correct,
   2 marks for both correct**)

Grammar Test 3 – pages 8-10

1. tidied
   (**1 mark**)

2. **The** weather was awful yesterday.
   (**1 mark**)

3. Nadia gave <u>them</u> some presents.
   Harry really likes <u>these</u> teacups
   (**1 mark for 1 correct,
   2 marks for both correct**)

Answers

Answers

4. E.g. The woman was singing **very** loudly.
   (**1 mark for any sensible adverb**)

5. They are working hard.
   (**1 mark**)

6. The river flowed <u>under the bridge</u>.
   <u>After lunch</u>, they had a long nap.
   (**1 mark for 1 correct,
   2 marks for both correct**)

7. pronoun
   (**1 mark**)

8. <u>Our very cute puppy</u> barked cheerfully.
   Noun: puppy
   (**1 mark for correctly underlining the noun phrase, 1 mark for correctly identifying the noun**)

9. E.g. They go outside but Oliver stays indoors.
   (**1 mark**)

10. Callum wrote poems <u>when he was younger</u>.
    <u>Before I go home</u>, I need to go to the shop.
    (**1 mark for 1 correct,
    2 marks for both correct**)

Grammar Test 4 – pages 11-13

1. adjective
   (**1 mark**)

2. I have sent <u>many</u> postcards today.
   (**1 mark**)

3. Rina likes playing the drums.
   (**1 mark**)

4. theirs
   (**1 mark**)

5. We could <u>have</u> gone to the seaside instead.
   (**1 mark**)

6. We were late **because** we overslept.
   Although she was full, Jill still made a pizza.
   (**1 mark for 1 correct,
   2 marks for both correct**)

7.
	Noun Phrase	Preposition Phrase
an enormous hippo	✓	
over the fence		✓
before sunset		✓

   (**1 mark for each correct,
   up to 3 marks in total**)

8. Kabir has cleaned
   We have danced
   (**1 mark for 1 correct,
   2 marks for both correct**)

9. E.g. I haven't got any more peaches.
   E.g. Kim doesn't know anything about monkeys.
   (**1 mark for each sentence that uses Standard English, up to 2 marks in total**)

Grammar Puzzle – page 14

1. first thing in the morning — **S**
2. You should have seen it. — **U**
3. mine — **N**
4. preposition — **S**
5. until it got dark — **E**
6. She, they — **T**

The code word is: SUNSET.

Punctuation Test 1 – pages 15-17

1. I still <u>havent</u> managed to find the toys I lost earlier.
   (**1 mark**)

2. That unicyclist was absolutely incredible?
   (**1 mark**)

3. Jenny said ↑, I think the clocks go back soon ↑.
       ✓   ✓
   (**1 mark for both correct**)

4. Keshav recently visited Marco in <u>rome</u>. They hadn't met up since Marco left <u>england</u> seven years ago.
   (**1 mark for 1 correct,
   2 marks for both correct**)

Answers

5. Yesterday evening, I went to the theatre.
   (**1 mark**)
6. It's finally going to snow tonight.
   (**1 mark**)
7. Maya spent the day swimming in streams, walking through woods, sketching birds and listening to music.
   (**1 mark for 1 comma correct, 2 marks for both correct**)
8. We are going to Tracy's birthday party this weekend.
   (**1 mark for starting 'We' with a capital letter, 1 mark for adding an apostrophe in 'Tracy's'**)
9. Bears are impressive creatures, and many people find them fascinating. As a result, they often appear in myths and stories. // Polar bears are among the largest bears. They live in the Arctic Circle where they hunt both on land and in the sea. // Kodiak bears are also large and can weigh more than 650 kg. They live on a group of islands near Alaska. Unlike polar bears, they eat plants as part of their diet.
   (**1 mark for 1 correct, 2 marks for both correct**)
10. All About Bears
    (**1 mark**)

Punctuation Test 2 – pages 18-20

1. they
   (**1 mark**)
2. This is utterly delicious
   (**1 mark**)
3. E.g. I need to buy a bag of radishes, two floppy hats, nine bottles of ketchup and some pink pens.
   (**1 mark for 1 comma correct, 2 marks for both correct. If any commas are added incorrectly, e.g. before the final 'and', deduct 1 mark for each incorrect comma**)
4. Did Liam win his chess match earlier?
   Stacey wants to go shopping this week.
   How can we try to solve this problem?
   (**1 mark for each correct, up to 3 marks in total**)
5. The three <u>cats</u> water bowls always seem to be empty.
   You should have written: cats'
   (**1 mark for underlining the correct word, 1 mark for writing the word with an apostrophe correctly**)
6. "I'm going to watch the stars," said Zinhle.
   E.g. To show that Zinhle is speaking out loud.
   (**1 mark for both inverted commas correct, 1 mark for any sensible explanation**)
7. Because of the old milk, it smells bad in here.
   If the rain stops, the cricket might start again.
   (**1 mark for 1 correct, 2 marks for both correct**)
8. E.g. Percy the Pirate's Adventure
   (**1 mark for any sensible heading**)

Punctuation Test 3 – pages 21-23

1. Beth bought a frisbee, shoes and a hat.
   (**1 mark**)
2. It is Tilly's birthday party next Wednesday.
   (**1 mark**)
3. wouldn't
   we'll
   (**1 mark for 1 correct, 2 marks for both correct**)
4. Nigels' eyes were wide with shock.
   (**1 mark**)
5. She likes to travel — .
   Do you think Kate is funny — !
   What a brilliant show that was — ?
   (**1 mark for 1 or 2 correct, 2 marks for 3 correct**)
6. The panda always eats all of its bamboo.
   Mary thinks it's going to rain today.
   (**1 mark for 1 correct, 2 marks for both correct**)

Answers

Answers

7. Before the sun came up, Azgar went for a run.
   (**1 mark for starting 'Before' with a capital letter, 1 mark for a comma after 'up', 1 mark for a full stop after 'run'**)

8. E.g. Climbing Mount Everest
   (**1 mark for any sensible heading**)

9. "We've been walking for absolutely ages," moaned Mark.
   (**1 mark for both inverted commas correct**)

Punctuation Puzzle – page 24

Lara — My bag **doesnt** contain any secret **plan's**, special gadgets or**,** jam jars. (3 mistakes)

Luke — **what** is my bag like**.** **Its** got a hidden pocket**,** at the bottom that is full of grapes**"**. (5 mistakes)

Satoshi — After sunset_ my bag becomes invisible. This means it won't be stolen while I am asleep. (1 mistake)

Maeve — What a great bag I have**?** **Itll** play music to me if I say the secret word. (2 mistakes)

Petra — My bag has a parachute_ This is great**,** when **Im'** on an **Aeroplane**. (4 mistakes)

Spelling Test 1 – pages 25-27

1. city
   (**1 mark**)
2. Sunita had troubel deciding which socks to wear.
   (**1 mark**)
3. The puppy **mis**behaved all day.
   (**1 mark**)
4. I would've preferred to go to the beach.
   (**1 mark**)

5. 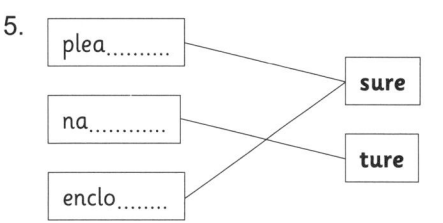 plea......... — sure
   na............ — ture
   enclo........
   (lines: plea→sure, na→ture, enclo→sure)
   (**1 mark for each correct, up to 3 marks in total**)

6. I love hearing my voice eko.
   (**1 mark**)

7. Millie won first prize in the school **science** contest.
   (**1 mark**)

8. discussion
   politician
   expression
   (**1 mark for each correct, up to 3 marks in total**)

9. Danny's sister, Julia, had always urged him to stay out of the attic. She claimed that there was a dangereous ghost lurking up there.
   One day, Danny decided to creep up to the attic to investigate. Although he felt nervous, he was also cureous to see what the ghost looked like.
   (**1 mark for 1 correct, 2 marks for both correct**)

Spelling Test 2 – pages 28-30

1. closeing
   (**1 mark**)
2. Zuko was allways the tallest student at school.
   (**1 mark**)
3. 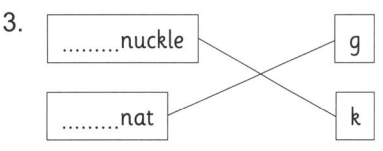 ....nuckle — k
   ....nat — g
   (lines cross: nuckle→k, nat... with k silent)
   (**1 mark for both correct**)
4. impossible
   inactive
   (**1 mark for 1 correct, 2 marks for both correct**)

57 Answers

Answers

5. The thief managed to steal the expensive **antique** clock.
   (**1 mark**)
6. The <u>veyns</u> in my arm are blue.
   <u>Thay</u> finished the quiz very quickly.
   (**1 mark for 1 correct,
   2 marks for both correct**)
7. finally
   dramatically
   (**1 mark for 1 correct,
   2 marks for both correct**)
8. The <u>pyramids</u> in Egypt are ancient.
   Steve knows so much about Greek <u>myths</u>.
   (**1 mark for 1 correct,
   2 marks for both correct**)
9. Freddie was full of **admiration** for his amazing friends. They had helped him with the **preparations** for his wonderful party.
   (**1 mark for 1 correct,
   2 marks for both correct**)

Spelling Test 3 – pages 31-33

1. I'm going to <u>wear</u> my favourite coat tonight.
   (**1 mark**)
2. I knew I'd bought the wrong <u>quontity</u>.
   (**1 mark**)
3. ou
   (**1 mark**)
4. limitting
   (**1 mark**)
5. scholar
   chorus
   (**1 mark for 1 correct,
   2 marks for both correct**)
6. confu→tion
   posse→ssion
   opera→tion (crossing lines to sion/ssion)
   (**1 mark for 1 or 2 correct,
   2 marks for 3 correct**)

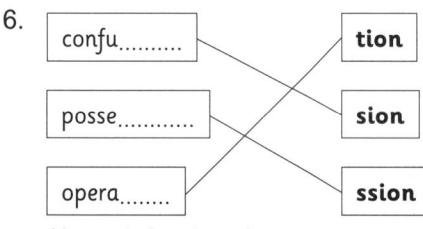

7. There will be a **crescent** moon tonight.
   (**1 mark**)
8. I carefully wrote the <u>address</u> on the envelope.
   We'll <u>probably</u> go for a swim later.
   It's hard to <u>describe</u> how delicious it was.
   (**1 mark for each correct,
   up to 3 marks in total**)
9. As soon as school was over, Amina and her friends raced to the **leisure** centre. They couldn't wait to try out the new **adventure** playground.
   (**1 mark for 1 correct,
   2 marks for both correct**)

Spelling Test 4 – pages 34-36

1. The animals cheer up the patients in the hospitel. ✓
   (**1 mark**)
2. Deb broke her <u>rist</u> when she fell out of the tree.
   (**1 mark**)
3. league
   (**1 mark**)
4. cian
   (**1 mark**)
5. glamorous
   envious
   (**1 mark for 1 correct,
   2 marks for both correct**)
6. He believes there will be an alien **invasion** tomorrow.
   (**1 mark**)
7. The vet gave my rabbit some **anti**biotics.
   Eve decided to **re**decorate the kitchen.
   I want to read the actor's **auto**biography.
   (**1 mark for 1 or 2 correct,
   2 marks for 3 correct**)
8. <u>canceling</u> — cancelling
   <u>profitted</u> — profited
   (**1 mark for 1 correct,
   2 marks for both correct**)

Answers

Answers

9. "It's not <u>fare</u>," Lena muttered with a groan. "It's pouring with rain and I can hardly see a thing through the <u>missed</u>. Why is the <u>whether</u> always terrible when we're on holiday?"
(**1 mark for each correct, up to 3 marks in total**)

Spelling Test 5 – pages 37-39

1. There is <u>nothing</u> but jam in the cupboards.
(**1 mark**)
2. My uncle lives in a small villadge in Scotland.
(**1 mark**)
3. il — perfect
   im — legal
   ir — relevant
(**1 mark for 1 or 2 correct, 2 marks for 3 correct**)
4. The giraffe had a surprisingly long ton**gue**. Matt put whipped cream onto the merin**gue**. The alarm went off and I spran**g** out of bed.
(**1 mark for each correct, up to 3 marks in total**)
5. I have trouble sitting still — I'm always **fidgeting**.
(**1 mark**)
6. My friend Barry has an amazing <u>imagineation</u>. He's always writing <u>extraordinaryly</u> exciting stories. I think he will be a famous author one day.
(**1 mark for 1 correct, 2 marks for both correct**)
7. moustache
(**1 mark**)
8. E.g. brochure
(**1 mark for any word where 'ch' is pronounced 'sh'**)

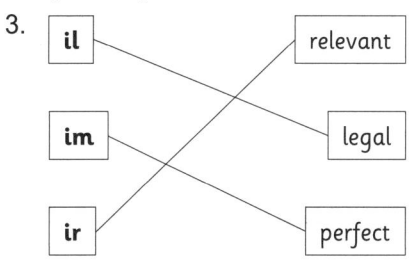

9. Christine **decided** to sleep in her tent.
The robin is a **regular** visitor to Nick's garden.
(**1 mark for 1 correct, 2 marks for both correct**)

Spelling Puzzle – page 40

You should have circled: skeme, dubble, Febuary, gentley, promiss, couragous, mashine, speshial, ordinery, preparacion

F	E	B	U	A	R	Y	I	O	Z	D	S
E	C	M	A	C	H	I	N	E	K	O	C
B	H	O	I	M	A	T	U	R	E	U	H
R	A	P	U	O	C	K	L	A	N	B	E
U	P	A	P	R	O	M	I	S	E	L	M
A	P	R	T	E	A	M	D	H	I	E	E
R	Y	G	B	A	L	G	E	N	T	L	Y
Y	L	Q	F	X	D	K	E	J	B	A	G
C	Y	R	A	N	I	D	R	O	F	N	N
S	P	E	C	I	A	L	O	E	U	V	W
I	L	R	A	Y	R	U	T	N	E	S	I
D	P	R	E	P	A	R	A	T	I	O	N

Mixed Practice Test 1 – pages 41-43

1. yung
(**1 mark**)
2. If we score again, we will win the match.
(**1 mark**)
3. yours and Hers
(**1 mark**)
4. Zack is building a boat.
They are washing the car.
(**1 mark for 1 correct, 2 marks for both correct**)
5. information
adoration
(**1 mark for 1 correct, 2 marks for both correct**)

Answers

6. I<u>tll</u> be amazing to see the turtles!
   It'll
   (**1 mark for underlining the correct word, 1 mark for writing the word with an apostrophe in the right place**)

7.
	Subordinating Conjunction	Co-ordinating Conjunction
I am tired but I need to stay awake.		✓
John will stay here until I pick him up.	✓	

   (**1 mark for 1 correct, 2 marks for both correct**)

8. <u>tenssion</u> — tension
   <u>injectsion</u> — injection
   <u>magisian</u> — magician
   (**1 mark for each correct, up to 3 marks in total**)

Mixed Practice Test 2 – pages 44-46

1. This car is one of a kind — it's completely <u>uniqe</u>.
   (**1 mark**)

2. On Tuesday, we are visiting a farm.
   (**1 mark**)

3. adjective
   (**1 mark**)

4. Yui told <u>him</u> to come home right away.
   (**1 mark**)

5. Nimit wants to hike up a mountain, go to a llama farm, play crazy golf and eat some crisps.
   (**1 mark for 1 correct, 2 marks for both correct**)

6. Amanda's fossil on the shelf
   our secret entrance behind the wall
   (**1 mark for 1 correct, 2 marks for both correct**)

7. The lioness hunted her pr......... — eigh
   An octopus has ....t legs. — ei
   The king r.........gned for a long time. — ey
   (**1 mark for 1 or 2 correct, 2 marks for 3 correct**)

8. The bears are eating the **campers** food.
   (**1 mark**)

9. Every evening, Nina rides her motorbike.
   (**1 mark**)

10. Shane loves to **exercise**. He regularly runs through the centre of town to the **library** and back again.
    (**1 mark for 1 correct, 2 marks for both correct**)

Mixed Practice Test 3 – pages 47-49

1. dge
   (**1 mark**)

2. How much longer do we have to wait**?**
   (**1 mark**)

3. controller
   commander
   (**1 mark for 1 correct, 2 marks for both correct**)

4. Have you seen <u>my</u> book anywhere? There are <u>some</u> letters here for Eva.
   (**1 mark for 1 correct, 2 marks for both correct**)

5. Tony plays the piano <u>when he stays with his uncle</u>.
   (**1 mark**)

6. Kieran said, "I'm going to plant a tree."
   (**1 mark**)

Answers

7. The ice cream parlour serves lots of flavours. You can get blackcurrant, bubblegum and even cabbage! They're all very tasty. // Last week, I went to the parlour, but it was closed. I had forgotten that they're shut during the winter. // When I am older, I will have my own ice cream parlour. It'll be open all year and will serve hot chocolate during the winter.
(**1 mark for 1 correct, 2 marks for both correct**)

8. E.g. the **happy** elephant **at the table**
(**1 mark for any sensible adjective, 1 mark for any sensible preposition phrase**)

9. Jason asked Nat to help him **measure** his furniture, a treasure chest and a brown **picture** frame.
(**1 mark for 1 correct, 2 marks for both correct**)

Mixed Practice Test 4 – pages 50-52

1. I still have many letters to hand out.
(**1 mark**)
2. mistery
(**1 mark**)
3. Sally and Bilal often argue and **dis**agree.
(**1 mark**)
4. Barney **has** talked to his children. We **have** eaten all of the broccoli.
(**1 mark for 1 correct, 2 marks for both correct**)
5. The bird is looking at its chicks.
(**1 mark**)
6. horribly
usually
(**1 mark for 1 correct, 2 marks for both correct**)

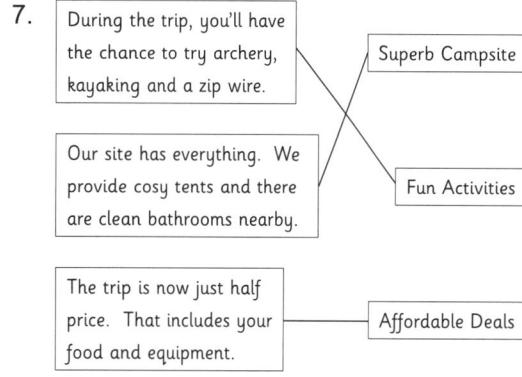

7.
- During the trip, you'll have the chance to try archery, kayaking and a zip wire. — Fun Activities
- Our site has everything. We provide cosy tents and there are clean bathrooms nearby. — Superb Campsite
- The trip is now just half price. That includes your food and equipment. — Affordable Deals

(**1 mark for 1 or 2 correct, 2 marks for 3 correct**)

8. Harriet should **have** passed me the ball. I've got to put all **those** books away.
(**1 mark for 1 correct, 2 marks for both correct**)

9. I had to go to the kemist after eating lunch at Gemma's house because her food made me ill. I was surprised because Gemma's a famous shef. She was very sorry.
(**1 mark for 1 correct, 2 marks for both correct**)

Mixed Practice Puzzle – page 53

Conjunctions:

You have found the mermaids' door, but can you open it? Many have tried to solve the puzzle and failed. If you wish to succeed, read our story.

Incorrectly spelt words:

Behind this door is an inmortality potion. We maid it for an impatient dragon who promised us tremendus powers. When she grew tired of waiting, she angryly blew our city to pieces with one mighty breathe.

Words that need apostrophes:

The dragons powerful, but she isnt smart enough to unlock the door. Its time to see if you have managed to uncover the mermaids secret.

The code to unlock the door is: 354

Progress Chart

You've finished all the tests in the book — well done!

Now it's time to put your scores in here and see how you've done.

	Grammar	Punctuation	Spelling	Mixed Practice
Test 1				
Test 2				
Test 3				
Test 4				
Test 5				

See if you're on target by checking your total marks for each test in the table below.

Mark	
0-7	You're not quite there yet, but don't worry — keep going back over the questions you find tricky and you'll improve your skills in no time.
8-11	Good job! You're doing really well, but make sure you keep working on your weaker topics.
12-14	Give yourself a huge pat on the back — you're a superstar!